21 DAYS

OF FASTING & PRAYER

FOR SPIRITUAL BREAKTHROUGH

TIFFANY K. JORDAN

21 DAYS

OF FASTING & PRAYER

FOR SPIRITUAL BREAKTHROUGH

TIFFANY K. JORDAN

21 Days of Fasting and Prayer for Spiritual Breakthrough

Published by Tiffany Jordan Ministries

Print Edition

Unless otherwise stated all Scripture quotations come from the King James version of the Bible.

Scriptures marked ESV® are from the ESV® Bible (The Holy Bible English Standard Version®). Adapted from the Revised Standard Version of the Bible. Permanent Text Edition (2016). Copyright © 2001 by Crossway, a publishing ministry of Good News Publishers. All rights reserved.

Scriptures marked NIV® are from the Holy Bible, New International Version®, NIV® Copyright ©1973, 1978, 1984, 2011 by Biblica, Inc.® Used by permission. All rights reserved worldwide.

Scriptures marked MSG are from The MESSAGE Bible Copyright © 1993, 1994, 1995, 1996, 2000, 2001, 2002 by Eugene H. Peterson Used by permission of NavPress Publishing Group.

For more information about Tiffany Jordan Ministries, please write us at:

380 E. St. Charles #231

Lombard, IL 60148

Visit our website: www.tiffanyjordan.co

CONTENTS

ACKNOWLEDGMENTS

First, I would like to thank God for the leading of the Holy Spirit that led me to do this fast, and His grace to finish it strong! Many lives were joined together through this act of obedience and many fasted for the first time. We saw lives come to Christ, captives set free, healings, signs, wonders and miracles.

For every person that met me faithfully to pray on Periscope and those that watched the replays, our lives will never be the same. I will forever be thankful for your commitment to seek the Lord and draw close to Him. The things that were prayed through during this time will have an eternal impact on your lives and future generations. Know that God heard every word, saw every sacrifice made, and He is pleased and faithful to heal and deliver. You will see the manifestation of the seeds sown!

INTRODUCTION

The Assignment

One morning in August of 2016, the Lord spoke to me and said, "Do a twenty-one day fast." It wasn't an unusual request for the Lord to ask of me, but what came after certainly was. He spoke very clearly and said, "Do it publicly and stand in faith with others through social media." Honestly, my first response was "No way!" as I have avoided certain platforms for not wanting to be out of the timing of the Lord. I heard the same thing again with the specific dates of September 1st through September 21st, which happened to be my birthday month as well. After much prayer and asking God why, I had to obey. The day before the start date, I posted a question on social media asking, "Who wants to fast and pray with me for twenty-one days?" Well, the response was definitely uncommon. I found that many people were hungry for more of God and wanted to be included.

It was not the beginning of the year where most people have made resolutions of getting their life right with God, going back to church, seeking God, etc. So, this was a remnant that God had been tugging on, and people just needed that extra support and push to take them into their promised land, their next level, or to give birth to what heaven had impregnated them with.

I sensed that many had gone through battle after battle. They had suffered spiritual miscarriages and abortions and were ready for change and results. The hunger that I sensed as I prayed coupled with the intensity in the spiritual realm was different than anything that I had ever experienced before but quite refreshing for me.

As I made it to my office, someone walked up and begin to confess that they had been avoiding coming to see me. They also mentioned that they had seen my morning's post on social media. I invited her into my office, and we talked about things that she had been dealing with in her life and how she knew God had spoken to me about the fast. During the meeting, deliverance and healing began. And God said, "This is why I need you to do the fast and prayer corporately. My people need a midwife." I wept! As I wept, realizing the needs of the people and the weightiness of the assignment, the burden came upon me to do the fast and prayer. To stand as a spiritual midwife involves assisting people in bringing forth the plans of God for their life, destroying yokes of bondages that have held them captive for decades, and causing individuals to walk in greater levels of intimacy with God.

With many prophecies spoken over my personal life concerning this year and this month, I entered into this fast fully persuaded that God had spoken and I had to obey! He specifically spoke concerning which social media platform He wanted me to use. As I stated earlier, I had been hesitant but with fear and trembling I obeyed the Lord despite what man might say or do.

The day before the fast, with minimal promoting, advertising or marketing of it, I went on the social media platform and announced that the fast would start the following day. I stated what time I would be praying each day, and talked about the purpose of fasting. Over one hundred people showed up the first day.

I remember being transparent about the fact that it wasn't me, as I preferred to fast in secret. But this was a fast that God Himself had chosen, and it was to be CORPORATE, for all those that were willing.

He promised to meet us there each morning as we met through the social media platform to pray and to seek Him. He promised that He would saturate us and there would be an anointing that would destroy yokes and lift burdens. He promised that there would be financial, healing, and relational miracles according to 3 John 2, *"Beloved, I wish above all things that thou mayest prosper and be in health, even as thy soul prospereth."*

I can honestly say that the Lord was true to His word and exceeded our expectations. The glory and power of God increased day by day until there was an open heaven, and many were drunk in the spirit, including me. I was overwhelmed by His faithfulness in the lives of His people.

The testimonies poured in daily and continued to increase. I have included some of the testimonies in the back of this book so that your faith can be increased during your time of fasting and prayer.

It is your inheritance to be intimate with God; fasting and prayer is a way to crucify the flesh and to be more in tune with the Spirit. An intentional pursuit through choosing to deny yourself of food and other pleasures of life, and consistently seeking God, will cause you to become more intimate with Him. Matthew 6:33, *"But seek ye first the kingdom of God and his righteousness; and all these things shall be added unto you."*

Choosing to fast is choosing to seek God and His way of living, being, and doing. It isn't seeking things but seeking Him who promised that as a result of our seeking, all other things would be added to us.

Thus, a corporate fast was called via my Periscope account for prayer each day. (*FYI, prayer scopes are still available for viewing so follow me @tiffanykjordan*).

What is Fasting?

A general definition of fasting is the voluntary abstinence from food for a period of time. The main purpose of a fast is to seek God and to develop a stronger relationship with Him. The early church consistently spent times in fasting and prayer. It was a

13

lifestyle. It should be the same for us.

We are not fasting to get God to do something, but we are fasting to draw close to Him. It's a way to silence the noise of our flesh and the different distractions that life can bring.

In every culture, people do some form of fasting. Fasting brings you into a closer commune and fellowship with the King of kings and the Lord of lords. We fast to honor God by choosing to spend quality time with Him and seek Him.

When we make a decision to fast, we are choosing to humble ourselves. It is an acknowledgment of our need for God. Fasting combined with prayer positions you to hear God clearly.

Though fasting is abstaining from food for a specific period of time, you can also fast from other things such as television, social media, telephone and anything that takes up a lot of your time. Some things in our life can become an idol without us knowing it, and it is during fasting that God reveals these things to us.

Fasting breaks the daily routine. It repositions and postures you to be sensitive to the Holy Spirit. Fasting requires you to decide to turn down the plate and usually activities that take up our time in order to draw nigh to God.

As we are fasting, we should also be meditating the Word of God and spending time in prayer. Giving up food alone is simply dieting. But as we fast we want to make it a point to seek God through reading the Bible, giving God praise and thanksgiving throughout the day, and spending quality time in prayer. Watching television, talking on the telephone, social media, etc. should be kept to a minimum if at all. We are saying, "Lord, we are turning away from everything that distracts us and looking unto Jesus Christ the author and finisher of our faith!"

During this twenty-one day journey, people were instructed to do the fast that they were most comfortable with. Overall, we recommended a Daniel fast, which consists of no meat, no sweets or bread. Daniel 10:3, *"I ate no pleasant bread, neither came flesh nor wine in my mouth, neither did I anoint myself at all, till three whole weeks were fulfilled."*

There are many types of fast but I will share just a few of them here.

Complete/Total: This fast is achieved when you go without eating or drinking foods and liquids, including water.

Absolute: In this fast, you abstain from all foods, but you can drink water. (Matthew 4:1-11)

Partial: This fast is accomplished when you eliminate certain kinds of solid foods and drinks from your normal daily diet as Daniel did. You can also achieve a partial fast in other ways such as abstaining from certain food until a certain time of day or omitting certain meals such as breakfast, lunch or dinner.

Corporate Fast: A corporate fast is where a group of people come together and decide to fast together at the same time. This type of fast releases unity and power as believers come together humbling themselves to seek the Lord.

There is usually a leader that is giving the direction and length of time for the fast. But the decision to comply and to join in is for each person to make individually. This is where the power of unity, submission to authority and hunger for more of the Lord is truly revealed. God shows up in these types of fasts. Signs, wonders and miracles flow easily.

What Fasting is Not

Fasting is not forcing God to do something. It is not for the purposes of manipulating God into giving you what you want or doing what you need Him to do. Also, fasting is not a way to get people to see how religious or how committed you are. Your fast should not be on display so that others can make comments about you. If that is someone's motivation, that person has already received their reward. Matthew 6:16 says, *"Moreover when ye fast, be not, as the hypocrites, of a sad countenance: for they disfigure their faces, that they may appear unto men to fast. Verily I say unto you, They have their reward."*

When you are fasting, it is not an excuse for you to be mean or irritable toward people because you have not eaten. Your demeanor should remain pleasant, and you shouldn't expect special treatment from those that are around you.

The fast allows us to develop a greater level of intimacy with God. It is an opportunity for us to remove distractions that hinder us in hearing and knowing what and when He is speaking. It is also a special time God can use to show us what is in our hearts so that we can be cleansed, purified, and washed by the water of the Word. Ephesians 5:26, *"That he might sanctify and cleanse it with the washing of water by the word."*

Journaling During Fasting & Prayer

A huge part of prayer is listening. It is important to write down what you hear while you are fasting and praying. Distractions will always come, so you must purpose in your heart to sit and listen and leave room for journaling in your prayer time.

Being quiet is where intimacy begins and when you discover the voice of God. God loves us and also loves talking to us. He is just waiting for us to be still. Many may say they are too busy to pray, but I say, "I cannot afford not to pray." It can become expensive living life and making decisions without waiting for direction from the Lord. So, as you are seeking God, be very intentional about keeping a journal and writing out in great detail what He reveals to you. It may be instructions, direction, clarity or just a single word. WRITE IT DOWN! Habakkuk 2:2 says, *"And the Lord answered me, and said, Write the vision, and make it plain upon tables, that he may run that readeth it."*

Meditating the Word

It is very important that during the fast, you spend time in the word. If you have specific things that you are believing God for during the fast, I would suggest that you write them out and have scriptures written next to those items with promises that assure you that what you are believing for is yours.

I also recommend reading the Bible. You can ask the Holy Spirit what to read. A good rule of thumb is to study out scriptures in the areas where you need development and growth. Throughout the day review them, speak them out, and even memorize them if possible. Joshua 1:8, *"This book of the law shall not depart out of thy mouth; but thou shalt meditate therein day and night, that thou mayest observe to do according to all that is written therein: for then thou shalt make thy way prosperous, and then thou shalt have good success."*

Time in Prayer

Spending quality time in prayer is critical to you experiencing an effective fast. The prayer should be geared toward seeking the Lord and drawing close to Him. It should also be spirit-led. If there is a specific thing that you need an answer to, bring it before the Lord during this time as well. Matthew 7:7, *"Ask, and it shall be given you; seek, and ye shall find; knock, and it shall be opened unto you."*

During your prayer time, make sure you spend as much time listening as you do making supplications and requests. God is always speaking, and as we silence ourselves before Him, He will speak and give us the direction, clarity and wisdom for the journey that we are embarking upon. John 10:27, *"My sheep hear my voice, and I know them, and they follow me."*

Divine Instructions During the Fast

Watch your words. Proverbs 18:21, *"Death and life are in the power of the tongue: and they that love it shall eat the fruit thereof."*

Don't defend yourself. 2 Chronicles 20:17, *"Ye shall not need to fight in this battle: set yourselves, stand ye still, and see the salvation of the Lord with you...."*

Don't get into strife. James 3:16, *"For where envying and strife is, there is confusion and every evil work."*

Stay in the presence of God. Psalm 16:11, *"Thou wilt shew me the path of life: in thy presence is fulness of joy; at thy right hand there are pleasures for evermore."*

Forgive immediately and apologize if necessary. Luke 23:34, *"Then said Jesus, Father, forgive them; for they know not what they do."*

Walk in the love of God at all cost. Romans 5:5, *"And hope maketh not ashamed; because the love of God is shed abroad in our hearts by the Holy Ghost which is given unto us."*

Guard your heart and the gates to your heart (your eyes, ears and mouth). Proverbs 4:23, *"Keep thy heart with all diligence; for out of it are the issues of life."*

Choose the fruit of the Spirit. Galatians 5:22, *"But the fruit of the Spirit is love, joy, peace, longsuffering, gentleness, goodness, faith, meekness, temperance: against such there is no law."*

WEEK ONE

Sanctify Yourselves

"And Joshua said unto the people, Sanctify yourselves: for to morrow the Lord will do wonders among you" (Joshua 3:5).

SANCTIFICATION means "to set apart as to declare holy; consecrate; free from sin; purify; make holy." God will set you apart and make you holy, purifying your heart. As you purpose in your heart to fast, you are setting aside a sacred time unto the Lord.

Sanctification cannot happen outside of God. As you commit yourself to Him, "He" will do the sanctifying. The longer we are in the presence of God, the more quickly the sanctification process takes place. As you enter the presence of God, you are blocking any and everything else out. Once you enter into His presence, it's easier to discipline our mind and gain clearance to enter into the Holy of Holies. Some call this the third heaven.

> *But God, who is rich in mercy, for his great love wherewith he loved us, Even when we were dead in sins hath quickened us together with Christ, (by grace ye are saved;) And hath raised us up together and made us sit together in heavenly places in Christ Jesus: That in the ages to come he might shew the exceeding riches of his grace in his kindness toward us through Christ Jesus.* Ephesians 2:4-6 KJV

We must allow God to sanctify us; we never want to try and sanctify ourselves. Sit back and relax and let God do the work. Jeremiah 17:9-10 KJV says that *"the heart is desperately wicked and He searches the heart."* Whenever we are in the presence of God, we should ask Him to search our hearts so that He can create in us a clean heart and renew a right spirit within us (Psalms 51: 10). Once God sanctifies us, He wants us to embrace holiness as a lifestyle not just during the fasting season. The Bible states in Proverbs 4:23, to *"guard your heart with all diligence."* The words *heart* and *spirit* can be used here interchangeably. As we allow God to sanctify us, we come into agreement with His truth. His truth says that we are not of the Kingdom of this world, but rather are of the Kingdom of God, being seated in heavenly realms in Christ Jesus, *"far above all rule and authority and power and domination, and above every name that is named"* (Ephesians 1:21).

The process of sanctification also includes CONSECRATION. Consecration calls for us to come out from among them (unbelievers) and cease from works of darkness. First Corinthians 6:17 says not to touch the unclean thing, set yourself apart. There must be a difference between the clean and unclean. Of course, this is a process, and this book can play a role in that process. Do not feel anxious, focusing on all the things that you need to change in your life. Truthfully, you do not know all the things you need to change. It is during times of consecration that the Spirit reveals these things to us and we receive a supernatural grace to transcend fleshly tendencies and to connect directly with the power of God. Let us purpose in our mind that once set apart we won't desire to go back. Remember to abide in the Word for it is the cleansing power of God (Ephesians 5:26).

Finally, the Bible says in 1 Peter 1:16, *"Be ye holy for I am holy."* The purification of your heart also means to forgive one another, love one another, and not allow offense to enter into our hearts. You should desire for the Holy Spirit to flow easily through you, not be hindered by a clogged up spirit. Once you've gone through the process of sanctification, then He'll receive you (1 Corinthians 6:17). Sanctification is a continual process, but know the more you set yourself apart; the more the anointing will flow in your life. The anointing is precious, so if you want it, sanctify yourself!

Day 1

Worship

"Then came Peter to him, and said, Lord, how oft shall my brother sin against me, and I forgive him? till seven times? Jesus saith unto him, I say not unto thee, Until seven times: but Until seventy times seven" (Matthew 18:21-22).

On the first day of the fast, we spent time praising and worshipping God. As we did, God began to speak. He led us into a time of repentance, forgiveness, and releasing others from our heart that may have harmed, hurt, or did us wrong in one way or the other. He desired that our hearts be pure and began a great cleansing and washing of hearts. God opened our eyes to see where we were holding on to unforgiveness and strife and any place where the enemy had an entrance to our lives.

We all repented and asked God to forgive us. We asked that He would create in us a clean heart and renew the right spirit within us. He began to bring people to our remembrance, and we called out their names and released them and the hurt of the pain that was caused by each incident. We forgave ourselves for holding it and asked God to heal us from emotional and physical wounds caused as we were holding grudges or bitterness in our hearts.

Healing and deliverance flowed as people began to release their names and the offense associated with them. During this time, we realized that we were not God and that we cannot hold people, as it hinders us not them. We forgave as He also has forgiven us. We asked God for His love to be shed abroad in our hearts in greater measure and for hearts that will see others the way He sees them.

Unforgiveness blocks the force of faith from working in our life. When we have unforgiveness in our hearts, we are not walking in love, as love covers and takes no account of a suffered wrong. Faith works by love, and it is impossible to please God without faith. No matter what has been done, God's forgiving grace and His love are available to us. It is our decision to tap into it and release others from our heart.

Forgiveness is definitely not the world's way of handling offense, especially when someone has hurt you. But the way of the Kingdom of God is to walk in the spirit and not the flesh. This is what sets us apart. We are called to be salt and light. Forgiving is an example of being light in a dark world where revenge is the immediate response to a wrong done. To forgive is an act of love. The desire to please God must be stronger than the desire for revenge, retaliation, hate, holding a grudge, etc. His love never fails!

Always remember that our lives are not our own and that we have been bought with a price.

Prayer Focus

_____

_____

_____

_____

What I Hear God Saying

_____

_____

_____

_____

What He is Leading Me to Do

_____

_____

_____

_____

Day 2

Repentance

"Have mercy upon me, O God, according to thy lovingkindness: according unto the multitude of thy tender mercies blot out my transgressions. Wash me thoroughly from mine iniquity, and cleanse me from my sin. For I acknowledge my transgressions: and my sin is ever before me" (Psalm 51:1-3).

On day two, we continued with the cleansing process of repentance, forgiving and releasing cares to God. We surrendered all that we are to Him. We continued to call on His name asking Him to search every fiber of our being as we postured our hearts to be cleansed and purged. We asked God to root up every

31

tree that He has not planted in us, and that it be replaced with the image and likeness of God.

We also asked God to search our hearts with the candle of the Spirit and for the Word of God be a mirror so that revelation comes to us concerning the areas that we need to change. We prayed and asked that the fallow ground be broken up and that God would, like a hammer smash to pieces those hardened areas of our heart and give us hearts of flesh. One thing that the Lord emphasized on this second day of the fast was giving up the right to be right.

I was amazed how people could continue to go deeper to discover things that had been plundered, hidden and buried within their hearts, but still continue to operate and ignore those things. Over a period of time, we can become calloused and desensitized to the unction and conviction of the Holy Spirit if we refuse to listen and obey. But if we intentionally seek God and ask Him for help, He will immediately begin to shine the light and answer the cries of His people.

Even though many were rebellious, prideful and harboring unforgiveness before the fast, as soon as they repented and began to cry out, God heard and began to answer.

The presence of the Lord was tangible, and His power flowed to each person that needed His deliverance and healing. God remains faithful to the righteous!

Cry out today, and ask the Lord to search your heart and show you the areas that you have been rebellious, prideful or full of self. He will show you and lead you into all truth. Ask the Holy Spirit, our Helper, to help you! He is faithful and just to forgive you and cleanse you of all unrighteousness.

Prayer Focus

_____

_____

_____

_____

What I Hear God Saying

_____

_____

_____

_____

What He is Leading Me to Do

_____

_____

_____

_____

Day 3

Sweet Surrender

"But the fruit of the Spirit is love, joy, peace, longsuffering, gentleness, goodness, faith, meekness, temperance: against such there is no law" (Galatians 5:22).

On day three we surrendered all that we are to God saying, "not our will, but His will be done." We asked God to show us things that we could not see before; asking for revelation and to receive insight to transform our mindsets, behaviors and habits. We confessed sins known and unknown and cast every care on Him because He cares for us.

Every burden we had was laid down before God, and we released the fire of God to burn up everything that was not like the true and living God. We cried out for holiness to be our portion and made a decision to turn away from all that would distract us and to look unto Jesus Christ who is the Author and Finisher of our faith. We asked for distractions and every hindrance to be removed and for LIGHT (revelation) to shine upon our hearts.

All of us desired for the fruit of the Spirit to be perfected in us as we PURSUED God and a deeper relationship with Him.

We were led to pray for children, schools and daycare centers as well as for churches and leaders. We prayed for salvation in every local assembly that would hold a worship service and for a spirit of evangelism to be released and cried out for the salvation of our loved ones.

We prayed also for the eradication of the spirit of religion and an invasion of the Kingdom of heaven manifesting miracles, signs and wonders. We decreed that intercessors would be raised up and released strength to those that are called to intercede. We bound the spirit of python that hinders the prayer lives of God's people and asked God to impregnate us with a burden for what heaven is desiring to release into the earth realm.

After reminding God of His promise to deliver us and our seed, we declared that the spirit of poverty is broken and commanded the blessing on our lives for favor, increase and abundance. We stood in faith for supernatural eradication of debts and God's overflow believing God to heal, deliver and to set every captive FREE!

Prayer Focus

_____

_____

_____

_____

What I Hear God Saying

_____

_____

_____

_____

What He is Leading Me to Do

_____

_____

_____

_____

Day 4

Agitation, Frustration and Negativity

"But thanks be to God, which giveth us the victory through our Lord Jesus Christ" (1 Corinthians 15:57).

Day four of our fast fell on a Sunday. We don't pray together on Periscope on Sundays but this particular Sunday we were instructed to spend time with God and seek Him alone. I happened to also be traveling that day but stayed in a posture of listening for the Holy Spirit to speak and send forth clarity, revelation, divine instructions and wisdom.

I personally had many things in prayer before the Lord, but truly desired the counsel of the Lord and His perfect will to be established. I inquired of Him concerning the matters that were on my heart as I know that He had the answer before the foundation of the world. With my heart, I sought Him, and verbally communicated with Him asking for light in the areas that still seemed unclear. I was reminded of how David constantly inquired of the Lord, and God would always answer him and give him divine instructions.

Agitation, frustration, and negativity are the enemies to spiritual clarity. Problems and questions can sometimes create such fearfulness in the hearts of many, but there is a peace that comes when we ask God specific questions and include Him in all of our decisions before making a move. It is especially comforting when He answers and gives the green light with a sure confirmation in your heart (spirit) about a situation. You are able to move forward full of faith knowing that God is with you. If God is with you, the victory is already guaranteed!

Prayer Focus

_____

_____

_____

_____

What I Hear God Saying

_____

_____

_____

_____

What He is Leading Me to Do

_____

_____

_____

_____

Day 5

Put On the Whole Armour

"Finally, my brethren, be strong in the Lord, and in the power of his might. Put on the whole armour of God, that ye may be able to stand against the wiles of the devil" (Ephesians 6:10-11).

Today seemed to shift into a level of spiritual warfare, as we went deeper. We asked God to unclog our ears to hear, and to sharpen our discernment. We also put on the full armour of God being led by the Holy Spirit. We know that we do not wrestle against flesh and blood, but against principalities, powers, rulers of darkness of this world, against spiritual wickedness in high places (Ephesians 6:12).

For day five, we put on the FULL ARMOUR of God according to Ephesians 6:13-17. We asked to be skillful with the sword of the spirit which is the Word of God asking God to help us in every situation that we would encounter throughout our day. We petitioned for Him to help us with our responses in conversations and situations. We asked for help with the words that come out of our mouths for we know that life and death are in the power of the tongue. We made a decision to speak life, knowing we needed the divine assistance of the Holy Spirit to help us in this endeavor. We prayed, "May our words edify, encourage and empower those that you bring across our path."

We prayed in faith, declaring that God was arising and that every enemy was scattering. We spent time binding the plans of the enemy and every covert and overt activity while loosing the plans of God to be established. As a group, we pulled down strongholds and took into captivity every thought contrary to the will and plan of God for our lives.

We asked for the mind of Christ and for our thoughts to be in line with the Word of God. We bound idle thoughts and thoughts that would cause us stay stagnant or in a place where we could not fully receive the promises of God.

We all recognize that God's wisdom is essential for our complete success; therefore, we asked for keys to unlock the secrets of the Kingdom of heaven.

Prayer Focus

_____

_____

_____

_____

What I Hear God Saying

_____

_____

_____

_____

What He is Leading Me to Do

_____

_____

_____

_____

Day 6

Making Melody in our Hearts

"Trust in the Lord with all thine heart; and lean not unto thine own understanding. In all thy ways acknowledge him, and he shall direct thy paths" (Proverbs 3:5-6).

"Wherefore he saith, Awake thou that sleepest, and arise from the dead, and Christ shall give thee light. See then that ye walk circumspectly, not as fools, but as wise, redeeming the time, because the days are evil...be filled with the Spirit, speaking to yourselves in psalms and hymns and spiritual songs, singing and making melody in your heart to the Lord; giving thanks always for all things unto God and the Father in the name of our Lord Jesus Christ; submitting yourselves one to another in the fear of God" (Ephesians 5:14-16, 18-21).

On day six of the fast, God instructed me to add music to the time of prayer on Periscope. The prophetic minstrel met me in the place of prayer. God said that if I would obey, He would bring supernatural increase. As we prayed, the Lord showed up in a way that was tangible.

I also noticed that the demonic forces increased as well. We prayed with power and just as He promised increase manifested in more ways than one. The first notable increase was the number of people that were tuned in for prayer. It went from a couple of hundred to a few thousand! God remains faithful. The lesson here was whatever He tells you to do—do it. Also, that He is God all by Himself and He can increase you whenever and however He chooses. We don't have to look to man, but our trust must be in the Lord.

As you seek the Lord today, ask Him to reveal your purpose—"your place of grace." I remember that on the prior day, I asked God to reveal my place of grace and He revealed it to me. And as I obeyed with the divine instruction, He brought forth the increase that no man could take credit for.

Prayer Focus

_____

_____

_____

_____

What I Hear God Saying

_____

_____

_____

_____

What He is Leading Me to Do

_____

_____

_____

_____

Day 7

Obedience

"And having in a readiness to revenge all disobedience, when your obedience is fulfilled" (2 Corinthians 10:6).

I was traveling on day seven of the fast, but it was important to get time in with the Lord. Obedience is and always will be a key to divine relationship with the Lord. As we obey Him, He can trust us with more. To whom much is given much is required. It didn't seem convenient to pray on Periscope while traveling, but I did it anyway.

We all prayed for direction and clarity, and we acknowledged that we could do nothing without God asking for Him to reveal His plan.

We then shifted into a time of commanding where we commanded all that pertains to our life to begin to come to us in abundance. We called forth money, resources, gainful employment, divine health, marriages, fruitful relationships and much more.

We declared that fear would not rule our lives. But we would rise up in boldness and obedience to the Word and to the voice of the Lord. We also decreed that even when we are uncomfortable, we would obey, step out and move forward knowing that God was backing us up!

Prayer Focus

_____

_____

_____

_____

What I Hear God Saying

_____

_____

_____

_____

What He is Leading Me to Do

_____

_____

_____

_____

WEEK TWO

PROPHETIC RELEASE:
Restoration, Elevation, Acceleration

"Is not this the kind of fasting I have chosen: to loose the chains of injustice and untie the cords of the yoke, to set the oppressed free and break every yoke? Is it not to share your food with the hungry and to provide the poor wanderer with shelter – when you see the naked, to clothe them, and not to turn away from your own flesh and blood? Then your light will break forth like the dawn, and your healing will quickly appear; then your righteousness will go before you, and the glory of the Lord will be your rear guard" (Isaiah 58:6-8 NIV)

Prophetically, I speak to you the utterance of the Lord. Prepare yourself for the blessing comes quickly, and you must be prepared that the magnitude of it does not overwhelm you. Strengthen your nets. Expand your capacity. Call together your helpers. Get your bank accounts in order. Organize your home and your business affairs. Bring yourself into optimal health. Bring your appearance up as the Lord will bring you before great men. Do everything that you need to do to manage the overflow. It comes quickly. Be prepared, thus says the Lord.

Furthermore, recognize that the Lord has chosen this fast and I hear three words echoing in the spirit, RESTORATION, ELEVATION, and ACCELERATION. These pleasant promises come with purpose, for as you commit to this fast and the sanctification of your life the Lord will give you deep revelation into His priorities for your life. The first step that He tells you to take will be connected to his priority. You will find that your steps will be directed by revelation, but they will be fueled by faith. As you press in fasting and prayer, you will feel the power of God, and it will manifest in three pronounced ways.

1. CLARITY
2. BOLDNESS
3. STRENGTH

You will begin to feel moments of clarity initially. Your spiritual vision and hearing will clear up. Soon revelation will increase, and divine inspiration will flow. Thoughts that you know did not originate in your own mind will come one after the other. It would be wise to purchase a journal to keep beside your bed, in the kitchen, restroom, or even at work or church. You may choose to use your phone to record downloads from the Spirit, especially when driving.

RESTORATION

Agreement plays a huge role in the restorative process. You're being unified in your spirit, soul, and body. You are being made whole in Christ Jesus, by way of the Holy Ghost. You are becoming single-minded. Once the curse is removed, and the blessing comes upon you, you have been restored. The enemy holds no place in your spirit, soul, or body. Your entire threefold being is now occupied by the Holy Ghost when restoration comes. You have been restored back to God, made in His image and likeness. It's a transformation that comes to you. As the Bible says in Romans 12:2, *"...be ye transformed by the renewing of your mind."* When restoration hits you, every relationship will be restored as well. First and foremost, your relationship with Jesus Christ is made whole then your marriages and other personal relationships.

ACCELERATION

Strength can be directly connected to acceleration. You can realign your strength and faith in God through fasting and prayer. The Bible says in Ephesians 6:10, *"Finally, my brethren, be strong in the Lord, and in the power of his might."* Also, Job 17:9 states, *"The righteous also shall hold on his way, and he that hath clean hands shall be stronger and stronger."* You have to stand in righteousness for the Bible says in Proverbs 14:34, *"Righteousness exalteth a nation...."* As your strength increases, acceleration will be your outcome. Visualize the hurdler, jumping like a gazelle over each hurdle. What do you see? You see long sleek muscles. You see shear strength and graceful, perfect form. What is the result? Speed! Expect momentum as you have never experienced before.

ELEVATION

To elevate is to lift up. According to Ephesians 2:6, God has "already" raised us up with Christ and seated us together in heavenly places in Christ Jesus. Through prayer, the revelation of "high places" will cause a manifestation of promotions, divine favor, the restoration of marriage, increased power in the Spirit, mental enlightenment, glory in your countenance, finances, work—everything!

The word of God confirms these three words even more.

RESTORATION

"And I will restore to you the years that the locust hath eaten, the cankerworm, and the caterpiller, and the palmerworm, my great army which I sent among you" (Joel 2:25).

ACCELERATION

"'Yes indeed, it won't be long now.' God's Decree. 'Things are going to happen so fast your head will swim, one thing fast on the heels of the other. You won't be able to keep up. Everything will be happening at once—and everywhere you look, blessings! Blessings like wine pouring off the mountains and

hills. I'll make everything right again for my people Israel:' *'They'll rebuild their ruined cities. They'll plant vineyards and drink good wine. They'll work their gardens and eat fresh vegetables. And I'll plant them, plant them on their own land. They'll never again be uprooted from the land I've given them.' God, your God, says so"* (Amos 9:13-15 MSG).

ELEVATION

"Humble yourselves in the sight of the Lord, and he shall lift you up" (James 4:10).

Day 8

I Am that I Am

"And God said unto Moses, I Am That I Am: and he said, Thus shalt thou say unto the children of Israel, I Am hath sent me unto you" (Exodus 3:14).

On day eight, as we entered into the presence of God with praises and thanksgiving we lifted up the name of Jesus. Philippians 2:10 declares, *"that at the name of Jesus every knee should bow, of things in heaven, and things in earth, and things under the earth."* We released that matchless name and cleared the atmosphere. It arrested every force trying to infiltrate our time of prayer.

We began to break strongholds coming against spirits of deception, confusion, generational curses, witchcraft, sorcery and divination and we released the Blood of Jesus, the name, the Spirit of Truth commanding every thought to be taken captive to the obedience of Christ.

We commanded every tree that the heavenly Father hasn't planted to be rooted out. We also declared that we are redeemed from every curse and entered into a time where we all declared "I AM."

Begin to say your I Am's daily. Create your world by declaring your I AM!

I AM Blessed

I AM Healthy

I AM Wisdom

I AM Delivered

I AM Holy

I AM Wealthy

I AM Righteous

I AM Apostolic

I AM Prophetic

I AM a World Changer

I AM a History Maker

I AM an Agent of Change

I AM the Head

I AM the Lender

I AM Favor

I AM an Influencer

Prayer Focus

_____

_____

_____

_____

What I Hear God Saying

_____

_____

_____

_____

What He is Leading Me to Do

_____

_____

_____

_____

Day 9

Harvest

"And I will make thy seed to multiply as the stars of heaven, and will give unto thy seed all these countries; and in thy seed shall all the nations of the earth be blessed" (Genesis 26:4).

On day nine, we acknowledged that it was the ninth day of the ninth month. Nine is the number of harvest; therefore, we declared it was a month of birthing!

We were led into a time of intercession for our children. We lifted up every child and youth to God. We declared that they would serve the Lord all the days of their lives and put God in remembrance of His Word that promises that the seed of the righteous shall be delivered. (Proverbs 11:21)

We covered our children and youth wherever they were and asked God to give them a divine encounter. We commanded every ungodly soul tie to be broken and for the plans of God to be fulfilled. We prayed for their protection and released the angels of the Lord to encamp around about them.

We then thanked God for supplying the needs of our children, as He is our only source. We declared their healing and deliverance for any and all afflictions.

There was a definite shift toward the end of the prayer. It was prophesied that a "Greater Works" anointing was being released. That God shall work His miracles through our hands producing big projects, building and planting organizations all over the world. I saw God opening up specific nations and locations during the prayer, and we called them out by name. These were all the places that God desires to go into with the gospel.

We declared "OPEN UP"!

Philippines	Singapore	China	Bermuda
Guatemala	Russia	Brazil	India
Australia	Canada	France	Cuba
Costa Rica	Germany	Tanzania	Mexico
Japan	Saudi Arabia	Finland	Haiti
Spain	South Africa	Ghana	Honduras
Turkey	Iceland	China	

Prayer Focus

_____

_____

_____

_____

What I Hear God Saying

_____

_____

_____

_____

What He is Leading Me to Do

_____

_____

_____

_____

Day 10

The Holy Spirit, Our Helper

"But the Comforter, which is the Holy Ghost, whom the Father will send in my name, he shall teach you all things, and bring all things to your remembrance, whatsoever I have said unto you" (John 14:26).

This was the halfway mark. We asked God to help us, and we called upon the Holy Spirit, our "helper." We asked for help in every area of our lives and to be able to help others. We prayed for guidance from the Holy Spirit and for His direction to help us understand the Word of God as we sit to read the Scriptures.

With surrendered hearts, we cried out and honored the Lord admitting how much we need His help. Our heart's cry was for Him to help us to walk in love, speak the Word only and to walk in the Spirit. We submitted to God and asked Him to help us to resist the devil because His Word says he will flee from us.

We gave God permission to have His way in our lives as we knew that He knows what's best for us. We yielded to the Holy Spirit and declared that we are on the frequency of heaven asking for the eagle's eye to see things ahead of time. We asked God to sharpen our discernment.

After that, we released a spirit of faith and declared we were doers of the Word and not hearers only. We decreed that we walk by faith and not by sight and continued to call things that be not as though that already are. The Holy Spirit did not let us down. He showed up and manifested in a very tangible way.

We released fire on the enemy, and on the enemies of our soul commanding everything that isn't like God to be burned in Jesus' name.

Prayer Focus

_____

_____

_____

_____

What I Hear God Saying

_____

_____

_____

_____

What He is Leading Me to Do

_____

_____

_____

_____

Day 11

Trust God

"Trust in the Lord with all thine heart; and lean not unto thine own understanding. In all thy ways acknowledge him, and he shall direct thy paths" (Proverbs 3:5-6).

This day started off being what I thought was normal, but prophetically I sensed something happening. It was a crossing over point in the realm of the spirit. I sensed divine partnerships and connections coming together but also sensed strong resistance from the enemy that would try to block, distract, and cause the desires of heaven to be delayed. I pressed in and moved forward. Each time there was resistance throughout the day, and there was much, I made bold steps of faith to witness to the lost, talk about the goodness of God in every environment, and walk as light among those that were in darkness.

My circumstances did not determine my attitude. I chose to be thankful to God each step of the way. There was a pressing that was necessary to get through the day, but I was confident that God was with me. I didn't let things steal my joy, even though there was great opportunity to do so. My trust and faith in God were being stretched because Scripture says we go from faith to faith and from glory to glory.

At the end of the day, I reflected on the grace of God. There were things that God revealed and exposed in order to bring order and structure. I was challenged to take care of areas in my life that needed to be brought into alignment with the prayers that had gone forth. We pray and we never know how God is going to do it, but if our trust is totally in Him, we will not be moved when things happen that make us feel uncertain.

God is there all the time, in the midst of it all, causing things to work out for our good. As we put our trust in Him and lean not on our own understanding, acknowledge Him in all of our ways, He will bring clear direction to our path.

Prayer Focus

_____

_____

_____

_____

What I Hear God Saying

_____

_____

_____

_____

What He is Leading Me to Do

_____

_____

_____

_____

Day 12

Let There Be Light

"Casting all your care upon him; for he careth for you" (1 Peter 5:7).

We prayed today and asked God for spiritual understanding according to Ephesians 1:18, *"The eyes of your understanding being enlightened; that ye may know what is the hope of His calling, and what the riches of the glory of His inheritance in the saints."*

We asked for and received the wisdom of God and declared that His wisdom is bringing us honor and giving us a wreath or crown of glory. We asked for the key to unlock the wisdom that comes from above declaring that as we walk in the wisdom of God, we will guard it because it is through His wisdom that we make wise decisions.

We declared that all of our ways are established, and we live and walk purposely and accurately according to the plan of God. We decreed that our steps are ordered by God, and our paths are shining brighter and brighter as we step.

The group then made bold declarations that WE ARE WISE. We are who God says we are, we have what the Word says we can have, and we can do what the Word says we can do. By faith, we do not stagger in unbelief, but we are strong in faith. We thanked God for the spirit of faith being released and that we call things that be not as though they already are. We have faith to speak to every circumstance and command every mountain to be removed and cast into the sea. Our faith is causing the enemy to stay at bay. Our faith is the victory that overcomes the world. We commanded every wall that would stand before us to come down!

Everyone was in agreement believing that our faith is working on our behalf and circumstances are coming into alignment with the will of God. Through this time of prayer and fasting, I believe that we are single-eyed and full of light, standing and declaring that we shall have what we say. As we speak life, we cancel death. As a group, we declared victory in every situation in our lives: marriages, finances, education, health, children, salvation, etc. In the end, we released our cares to Him, for we know that He cares for us.

Now you RELEASE EVERY CARE calling them out by name!!

Prayer Focus

_____

_____

_____

_____

What I Hear God Saying

_____

_____

_____

_____

What He is Leading Me to Do

_____

_____

_____

_____

_____

Day 13

All Things Be Made New

"The seed of the righteous shall be delivered" (Proverbs 11:21b).

During prayer time on day thirteen, we began by lifting up the name of Jesus, the name above every name. I sensed a strength in the spirit, and that many had received victory and breakthrough. We had many testimonies and used those to encourage and strengthen us to go forward on our journey.

We declared that we are walking out of the realm of failure and defeat and walking in dominion, by faith and not by sight and in total victory.

We declared that we are redeemed from every curse and translated into the Kingdom of His dear Son. We thanked God for making us a new creation and declared that old things are passed away and that all things are being made new.

We, as a group, commanded all things to be made new and that we forget those things that are behind us reaching forward to the things that are ahead. We thanked God for success and progress declaring that angels are assisting us to take mighty leaps of faith and that we will not be stagnant. We then released a spirit of faith and that by faith we shall take what belongs to us. We began to take our inheritance: long life, our children out of the hand of the enemy, our ministries, our businesses, our health, our resources and our wealth. We declared that we are taking up our beds and we are walking!

We continued to declare that we are not waiting for someone to pick us up, but that we have the courage to take it by faith. The group then snatched every child out of the grips of the enemy, declaring deliverance for the seed of the righteous.

CALL EVERY CHILD OUT BY NAME! Release their name unto God, and thank Him that salvation is coming to every child, daughter, son, niece, nephew.

The group began to sever every ungodly soul tie and alliance and commanded every ungodly influence to be removed. We declared reconciliation of children to their parents, called them back to their homes, and into the Kingdom of God. We sent the Word that they are accepting Jesus Christ into their hearts and declaring with their voices that they want to be saved and that Jesus Christ is their Lord and we covered them with the Blood of Jesus and cried out for mercy.

We thanked God for fighting on our behalf and on behalf of our children and families releasing the Word, the Blood and the name of Jesus. We declared that wherever they are God would deliver them and give them a divine encounter. We canceled and broke every generational cycle, curse and all forms of witchcraft in operation against our children and thanked God for divine protection.

Our children shall be taught of the Lord, and great shall be their peace. They shall dwell in the house of the Lord all the days of their lives.

Prayer Focus

_____

_____

_____

_____

What I Hear God Saying

_____

_____

_____

_____

What He is Leading Me to Do

_____

_____

_____

_____

Day 14

By His Love, It's Already Done

"Forever, O Lord, thy word is settled in heaven" (Psalm 119:89).

Day fourteen brought us into a time of praise and thanksgiving unto the Lord. We began to thank God for His Word, and that His Word was producing the seed of righteousness within us. We thanked God that His Word is a lamp to our feet and a light to our path, that our steps are ordered by the Word and that we make decisions that are in alignment with the Word.

We all proclaimed that we love the Word and thanked God that every promise in Him is yea and amen. We asked the Holy Spirit to lead and guide us into all truth. Everyone declared that we are confident that the Word is true, and we have made it the standard by which we live. The Word gives us wisdom, clarity and direction. The Word settles every question, and we choose to come into agreement with the Word. As a group, we chose to disagree with any thought, condition or circumstance that is contrary to the Word of God.

We refused to accept poverty, pride, jealousy, envy, strife, adultery, idolatry, etc. We boldly declared that our heart is fixed on the solid foundation of the Word. We committed to living and being governed by the Word. We released a spirit of obedience and rejected rebellion. As we committed ourselves to the Word, we also commit to obey God, for they are one. We decided to obey Him and to walk in humility. As we clothed ourselves with humility and renounced pride and arrogance, we were submitted to the Word, that shifts, heals, brings order and judges the very thoughts, purposes and intents of our hearts. We committed to testing our own actions and not compare ourselves with anyone. We made a commitment to hide God's Word in our hearts that we not sin against Him.

We then clothed ourselves with kindness, the love of God, patience, gentleness, longsuffering and asked for His help to choose the fruit of the spirit over the lusts of the flesh. We asked for His help to crucify it daily. We forgave all of those with grievances against us and asked for help to not rehearse or remember the sins that have been committed against us. We refused and rejected unforgiveness and refused to have iniquity in our heart because we need God to hear us. We chose to love and to pursue peace with all men allowing the love of God to be shed abroad in our hearts on this fourteenth day of prayer and fasting. Taking no account of suffered wrongs, we joyously released a spirit of liberty in Jesus' name!

Prayer Focus

_____

_____

_____

_____

What I Hear God Saying

_____

_____

_____

_____

What He is Leading Me to Do

_____

_____

_____

_____

WEEK THREE

Increase

The Word carries energy and the power to serve as a catalyst to increase. The following scriptures support the fact that God is a God of increase. When you read them, you will sense the power of God increasing you. As the Bible says the Word of God is both Spirit and Life, you will sense God's life-giving Spirit quickening you through His Word. The Word of God is also God Himself as it is written; *in the beginning was the Word and the Word was with God and the Word was God.* Keep these thoughts in mind as you read and meditate His Word.

Isaiah 54:2 ESV

Enlarge the place of your tent, and let the curtains of your habitations be stretched out; do not hold back; lengthen your cords and strengthen your stakes.

2 Corinthians 9:10 ESV

He who supplies seed to the sower and bread for food will supply and multiply your seed for sowing and increase the harvest of your righteousness.

1 Chronicles 4:9-10 ESV

Jabez was more honorable than his brothers; and his mother called his name Jabez, saying, "Because I bore him in pain." Jabez called upon the God of Israel, saying, "Oh that you would bless me and enlarge my border, and that your hand might be with me, and that you would keep me from harm so that it might not bring me pain!" And God granted what he asked.

Psalm 115:14-15 ESV

May the Lord give you increase, you and your children! May you be blessed by the Lord, who made heaven and earth!

Luke 6:38 ESV

Give, and it will be given to you. Good measure, pressed down, shaken together, running over, will be put into your lap. For with the measure you use it will be measured back to you."

Mark 4:24 ESV

And he said to them, "Pay attention to what you hear: with the measure you use, it will be measured to you, and still more will be added to you.

Malachi 3:10 ESV

Bring the full tithe into the storehouse, that there may be food in my house. And thereby put me to the test, says the Lord of hosts, if I will not open the windows of heaven for you and pour down for you a blessing until there is no more need.

Genesis 26:12 ESV

And Isaac sowed in that land and reaped in the same year a hundredfold. The Lord blessed him.

Isaiah 65:24 ESV

Before they call I will answer; while they are yet speaking I will hear.

Psalm 119:32 ESV

I will run in the way of your commandments when you

enlarge my heart!

Proverbs 3:9-10 ESV

Honor the Lord with your wealth and with the firstfruits of all your produce; then your barns will be filled with plenty, and your vats will be bursting with wine.

Proverbs 19:17 ESV

Whoever is generous to the poor lends to the Lord, and he will repay him for his deed.

Psalm 18:36 ESV

You gave a wide place for my steps under me, and my feet did not slip.

Job 8:7 ESV

And though your beginning was small, your latter days will be very great.

John 3:30 ESV

He must increase, but I must decrease.

Psalm 115:14 ESV

May the Lord give you increase, you and your children!

Deuteronomy 1:11 ESV

May the Lord, the God of your fathers, make you a thousand times as many as you are and bless you, as he has promised you!

2 Samuel 22:37 ESV

You gave a wide place for my steps under me, and my feet did not slip.

Deuteronomy 19:7-9 ESV

Therefore I command you, You shall set apart three cities. And if the Lord your God enlarges your territory, as he has sworn to your fathers, and gives you all the land that he promised to give to your fathers—provided you are careful to keep all this commandment, which I command you today, by loving the Lord your God and by walking ever in his ways—then you shall add three other cities to these three.

Romans 13:8-10 ESV

Owe no one anything, except to love each other, for the one who loves another has fulfilled the law. For the commandments, "You shall not commit adultery, You shall not murder, You shall not steal, You shall not covet," and any other commandment, are summed up in this word: "You shall love your neighbor as yourself." Love does no wrong to a neighbor; therefore love is the fulfilling of the law.

Psalm 144:13 ESV

May our granaries be full, providing all kinds of produce; may our sheep bring forth thousands and ten thousands in our fields.

Ephesians 3:20 ESV

Now to him who is able to do far more abundantly than all that we ask or think, according to the power at work within us.

Matthew 25:26-30 ESV

But his master answered him, 'You wicked and slothful servant! You knew that I reap where I have not sown and gather where I scattered no seed? Then you ought to have invested my money with the bankers, and at my coming I should have received what was my own with interest. So take the talent from him and give it to him who has the ten talents. For to everyone who has will more be given, and he will have an abundance. But from the one who has not, even what he has will be taken away. And cast the worthless servant into the outer darkness. In that place there will be weeping and gnashing of teeth.'

1 Corinthians 3:6-7 ESV

I planted, Apollos watered, but God gave the growth. So neither he who plants nor he who waters is anything, but only God who gives the growth.

Exodus 34:24 ESV

For I will cast out nations before you and enlarge your borders; no one shall covet your land, when you go up to appear before the Lord your God three times in the year.

1 John 4:7-16 ESV

Beloved, let us love one another, for love is from God, and whoever loves has been born of God and knows God. Anyone who does not love does not know God, because God is love. In this the love of God was made manifest among us, that God sent his only Son into the world, so that we might live through him. In this is love, not that we have loved God but that he loved us and sent his Son to be the propitiation for our sins. Beloved, if God so loved us, we also ought to love one another.

Isaiah 9:7 ESV

Of the increase of his government and of peace there will be no end, on the throne of David and over his kingdom, to establish it and to uphold it with justice and with righteousness from this time forth and forevermore. The zeal of the Lord of hosts will do this.

Psalm 71:21 ESV

You will increase my greatness and comfort me again.

Deuteronomy 12:18-20 ESV

But you shall eat them before the Lord your God in the place that the Lord your God will choose, you and your son and your daughter, your male servant and your female servant, and the Levite who is within your towns. And you shall rejoice before the Lord your God in all that you undertake. Take care that you do not neglect the Levite as long as you live in your land. "When the Lord your God enlarges your territory, as he has promised you, and you say, 'I will eat meat,' because you crave meat, you may eat meat whenever you desire.

Genesis 9:27 ESV

May God enlarge Japheth, and let him dwell in the tents of Shem, and let Canaan be his servant.

Deuteronomy 32:13 ESV

He made him ride on the high places of the land, and he ate the produce of the field, and he suckled him with honey out of the rock, and oil out of the flinty rock.

Genesis 26:13-14 ESV

And the man became rich, and gained more and more until he became very wealthy. He had possessions of flocks and herds and many servants, so that the Philistines envied him.

Genesis 7:17 ESV

The flood continued forty days on the earth. The waters increased and bore up the ark, and it rose high above the earth.

Acts 16:4-5 ESV

As they went on their way through the cities, they delivered to them for observance the decisions that had been reached by the apostles and elders who were in Jerusalem. So the churches were strengthened in the faith, and they increased in numbers daily.

Joshua 1:8-10 ESV

This Book of the Law shall not depart from your mouth, but you shall meditate on it day and night, so that you may be careful to do according to all that is written in it. For then you will make your way prosperous, and then you will have good success. Have I not commanded you? Be strong and courageous. Do not be frightened, and do not be dismayed, for the Lord your God is with you wherever you go." And Joshua commanded the officers of the people.

Matthew 19:29 ESV

And everyone who has left houses or brothers or sisters or father or mother or children or lands, for my name's sake, will receive a hundredfold and will inherit eternal life.

Day 15

We Believe

"We having the same spirit of faith, according as it is written, I believed, and therefore have I spoken; we also believe, and therefore speak" (2 Corinthians 4:13).

On day fifteen, we lifted up the names of God and praised Him for who is. We declared our love for Him and thanked Him for first loving us. We thanked God for shedding his love abroad in our heart and thanked Him for the fruit of love, the agape love for Him and also for others. As believers, we filled this day declaring what we believe.

We proclaimed what we BELIEVE that Jesus Christ is Lord and that He is ordering our steps and leading us. We believe that the angels are assisting us, that heaven hears us when we pray, that the effectual fervent prayers of a righteous man avails much and that we can decree a thing and it will be established unto us. During this prayer time, we believe that the blessing of the Lord is bringing wealth to us adding no painful toil. We declared that the seed of the righteous shall be delivered and believed God for marriages made in heaven, that when a man finds a wife, he finds a good thing and obtains the favor of the Lord. We believe God is not a man that He should lie, nor the son of man that He should repent. We declared that He has favored us and called us out by name, that nothing can hurt us because we believe His Word. We believe in the finished work that was accomplished on the cross, that we are new creatures in Him and that old things have passed away and all things have become NEW.

We commanded a paradigm shift to bring us into divine alignment with the will of God. We came according to Psalm 40:7 that says of the volume in the book is written of us, that what God has for us this day is being fulfilled. We declared that every prophetic word spoken over us, every passage of scripture, every word that God spoke to us in secret is coming to pass. We believe the Lord, and therefore we speak it. We resisted and denied every lie, every seed that the enemy has planted through teachings, experiences, words, etc. and commanded it to be rooted out in Jesus' name. Deliverance is the children's bread, and we released deliverance. We commanded everything that is not like

God to come up and out. We commanded exposure and casting out of every demonic spirit, familiar spirit and generational curse and believed we have received it all!

Declare today what you BELIEVE!

Prayer Focus

_____

_____

_____

_____

What I Hear God Saying

_____

_____

_____

_____

What He is Leading Me to Do

_____

_____

_____

_____

Day 16

We Intercede

"Trust in the Lord with all thine heart; and lean not unto thine own understanding. In all thy ways acknowledge him, and he shall direct thy paths" (Proverbs 3:5-6).

We continued to pour out our hearts to God and asked that He continue to create in us a clean, pure heart and to renew the right spirit within us. We asked the Holy Spirit to continue to show us the areas that we need to correct, adjust, and to come higher. We came not asking for things but seeking first the Kingdom of God and God's way of living, being and doing, thanking Him that as we do, all things will be added unto us.

We asked for heightened discernment and a greater level of sensitivity to the Holy Spirit and the voice of God. We asked God to lead us and guide us every step of the way. We acknowledged that we need God and the divine counsel of the Lord.

We began to lift up leaders and covered every apostle, prophet, evangelist, pastor and teacher. We came against every compromising spirit and declared that we will not bow to Jezebel or eat at her table. We declared that we will speak up for what is right in the eyes of the Lord. We declared a spirit of prayer, thanksgiving and supplication would rest upon us.

We yielded to be intercessors that will pray in the will of God. We asked God to make us His midwives and committed to pray what heaven desires to bring forth. We surrendered to be the ones that God uses to stand in the gap and make up the hedge for others.

We commanded strongholds to be pulled down and broken. Strongholds of the mind, infirmity, manipulation, control, deception, divination, witchcraft and sorcery—we commanded all to loose their grip and loose their hold. We broke the power of the enemy allowing God to arise and every enemy to be scattered. We made a decree for the Word to rise on the inside of us and become flesh.

We asked for the anointing of Joseph to come upon us, the anointing of Daniel for ten times greater, the favor of Esther and the strength and courage of Joshua to go into our promised land. We thanked God for faith, love, and peace and a glorious day!

Prayer Focus

_____

_____

_____

_____

What I Hear God Saying

_____

_____

_____

_____

What He is Leading Me to Do

_____

_____

_____

_____

Day 17

We Declare

"But he answered and said, Every plant, which my heavenly Father hath not planted, shall be rooted up" (Matthew 15:13).

Day seventeen was a day of declaration. We entered into the presence of God in prayer through praise and thanksgiving unto Him and released the blood of Jesus and the name of Jesus. We released the name of Jesus into every situation and declared that His name was above every other name. His name is above diabetes, cancer, high blood pressure, arthritis, every sickness and disease. We bound the spirit of infirmity and released divine health and healing in Jesus' name declaring that by the stripes of Jesus we are healed!

We asked God to remove every distraction, and declared that no weapon formed against us would prosper. We declared that God is removing and eradicating all covert and overt activities from our lives. We declared that a thousand can fall at our side and ten thousand at our right hand, but it shall not come nigh us. We will not walk in deception or be confused. We will always know what is good versus evil.

We put our visions in the hand of the Lord and asked Him to show us what to do. We asked what should we create in this season and for His help, to be in His perfect will. We sought the Lord for His direction, understanding, clarity, answers and solutions.

We desired intimacy with the Lord, being thirsty for that relationship with Him. We wanted more of Him, more of His presence, more revelation and to be close to Him and to walk more like Him. We asked that every tree that the enemy has planted be rooted up and replaced with the image and likeness of God. We quenched every dart of the wicked one and declared that the mind of Christ is our portion.

Our final declaration this day was we are

Kingdom advancers, world changers and history makers in Jesus' name!

Prayer Focus

_____

_____

_____

_____

What I Hear God Saying

_____

_____

_____

_____

What He is Leading Me to Do

_____

_____

_____

_____

Day 18

We Hear

"Then the spirit took me up, and I heard behind me a voice of a great rushing, saying, Blessed be the glory of the Lord from his place" (Ezekiel 3:12).

Today was a day to spend time alone with the Father. I spent time seeking God for direction, clarity, and revelation. As I entered into the presence of the Lord through praise and thanksgiving, I began to call on the precious name of Jesus. The glory of God filled my kitchen, and I simply basked in it.

I heard the voice of the Lord speak clearly to me "the poor man's wisdom is despised, and his words are not heard." I opened my eyes and thought to myself, "surely this isn't God," because I wasn't asking about finances. I heard it a couple more times, and then I began to look for it in the Bible. I located the scripture in Ecclesiastes 9:16. I said wow! God spoke to me that He desires to teach His people financial prosperity.

I had no idea why the Lord was speaking this to me, but it was clear that it was His desire. His voice was confirmed through His Word. Never has anything been made so clear to me since I received my calling into ministry. God continued to instruct me to spend the last three days of the fast praying in the area of finances.

I took the instructions very seriously and spent the rest of the day seeking the Lord and in the Word of God. I made the announcement to those that had been standing in faith and we declared that we would obey the voice of the Lord.

I studied and meditated finance scriptures in preparation for the prayer time set for the next three days. I knew that God wanted to set us free financially and believed that we would see signs, wonders and miracles.

Prayer Focus

_____

_____

_____

_____

What I Hear God Saying

_____

_____

_____

_____

What He is Leading Me to Do

_____

_____

_____

_____

Day 19

We Increase

***"The blessing of the Lord, it maketh rich, and he addeth no
sorrow with it"*** (Proverbs 10:22).

Three more days to go and we are strong in the
Lord and the power of His might. I felt strong
physically, spiritually and emotionally. I also sensed the
strength of the those that were joining in doing the
corporate fast and prayer. God has been faithful, and we
continued to press in. We thanked Him for what He has
done so far and all that He was going to do.

Divine instructions were given by God to focus on
finances the last three days of the fast. We added an
evening time of prayer along with the morning prayer.

We prayed and lifted up our finances and declared that the spirit of debt is canceled from our lives. We lifted up every financial responsibility and believed God for supernatural eradication of debt and financial increase.

We commanded the Blessing on our lives and bound the spirit of poverty. We brought God into remembrance of His Word that wealth and riches are in our house and that He has given all things richly to enjoy. We declared sweatless victory in every financial situation.

We commanded every mountain to be removed and cast into the sea. We decreed Jubilee experiences and that we are holy millionaires, billionaires, and trillionaires. We declared financial miracles, creative ideas and witty inventions and multiple streams of income. We asked for revelation and declared LIGHT BE.

We thanked God for our gifts and declared that they are making room for us and bringing us before great men. God is our source, and we shall not want. We declared abundance, more than enough, grace and glory. We agreed that God is prospering our souls, our bodies, and finances according to 3 John 2.

Our confession on day nineteen was that God is advancing His Kingdom through us. We are His financiers. We will never beg nor borrow. We will lend to nations and are blessed to be a blessing. We are faithful tithers and we give and it is given unto us good measure pressed down shaken together and running over. (Luke 6:38)

We declared that the enemy will not destroy our seed nor our harvest. We declared that poverty is eradicated and we will never be broke another day of our life. Wealth and riches are in our homes and we leave an inheritance for our children's children.

We asked the Holy Spirit to help us to know how to use the power that God has given us to get wealth. As we hearken to the voice of God's Word, we know that all of these blessings are coming upon us.

Prayer Focus

_____

_____

_____

_____

What I Hear God Saying

_____

_____

_____

_____

What He is Leading Me to Do

_____

_____

_____

_____

Day 20

We Recover All

"Wealth and riches shall be in his house: and his righteousness endureth forever" (Psalm 112:3).

We continued to praise and thank God. We went in strongly for our financial freedom. We asked God for revelation of the Kingdom economy so that we can be good stewards of all that He gives us. We commanded supernatural eradication of all debts: student loans, mortgages, cars, credit cards, hospital bills, etc. We thanked God that favor, grace and mercy were our portion. We repented for any area where we have erred (not condemnation, but conviction).

We commanded a severing of the cord of poverty and declared that it would not affect us or the generations that are coming behind us. We pleaded the blood of Jesus over our finances and asked for the mind of Christ. We asked that not only we would understand the spiritual, but also the natural commands that we need to follow.

We asked for time management, ownership, stewardship, integrity and character as we handle our financial affairs. We asked for wisdom and declared that we would seek the Lord when increase comes in. We commanded the transfer of the wealth to come into our hands and that we are increasing more and more and stagnation and complacency are removed from our lives completely.

We declared more than enough, abundance and no lack, wealth and riches, increase and unlimited supply. We called forth money, land, real estate, gold and silver, royalties and dividends. We commanded a bumper crop on the good seeds that we have sown. We released angels to move and assist us in our Kingdom endeavors. Every spiritual and earthly blessing we commanded to come to us in abundance and we have nothing missing or broken. We proclaimed we are blessed in the city and the field.

We asked God to touch our minds and restore dreams and vision, purpose and destiny. To show us our identity and our place of grace and vision, which comes with provision. We also sowed seed as God poured out revelation on Kingdom economics.

We shall pursue, overtake and recover all!

Prayer Focus

_____

_____

_____

_____

What I Hear God Saying

_____

_____

_____

_____

What He is Leading Me to Do

_____

_____

_____

_____

Day 21

We Sow,
For We Know We Have Been Heard

"Behold, the days come, saith the Lord, that the plowman shall overtake the reaper, and the treader of grapes him that soweth seed; and the mountains shall drop sweet wine, and all the hills shall melt" (Amos 9:13).

The victorious finale! We ended strong and powerfully. God took us to another level of faith and glory. We celebrated for victories known and unknown. We gave God the highest praise with the fruit of our lips and out of the abundance of our hearts!

God was faithful during this time of prayer and fasting, and there have been many testimonies that have come forth. (See testimonies at the back of this book).

The Lord put a song in my spirit that spoke of rain, and while I sang, it began to rain outside my home. The glory of Lord began to fill my home and the prayer line. We worshiped the Lord and praised Him with a song.

Some of the lyrics to the song are:
"We've been praying....
We've been sowing....
Now we're crying, heaven send the rain."

The psalmist proclaimed that "seed only matters to those that have seed in the ground." We watered our Word seed, prayer seed and financial seed with praise, worship and the song of the Lord. What a glorious time in Him. We believe we've received every petition, request, declaration and prophetic utterance that has been released, proclaimed and prophesied during the twenty-one days.

We remain in faith that what God has promised shall be delivered unto us. Our faith will not be shaken, and we shall not be weary in our well doing but, we fully expect to reap the harvest and for God to do exceeding, abundantly above all that we have asked of Him. We are confident that we have prayed according to the will of God and that He has heard us. Therefore, we know that we have the petitions that we have asked of Him according to 1 John 5:14-15 in Jesus' name!

Prayer Focus

_____

_____

_____

_____

What I Hear God Saying

_____

_____

_____

_____

What He is Leading Me to Do

_____

_____

_____

_____

CONFESSION OF PRAISE

Father, I thank you and praise you for your faithfulness. You are my light and salvation, whom shall I fear or dread? You are more to me than life itself. You are great and greatly to be praised.

I lift my voice and my hands and I give you the glory that is due your name. I enter into your gates with thanksgiving and into your courts with praise and honor. Lord, you alone are worthy, you alone are holy. You rule and you reign over all.

You are the lover of my soul. You are the lifter up of my head. You are the King of kings and the Lord of lords. I will bless you at all times and your praise shall continually be in my mouth. I magnify and exalt your name. I yearn for you. I hunger and thirst for you Lord. You are mine and I am yours.

You are my shepherd and I thank you that I shall never want. You are the Truth, the Way and the Life. My trust is in you for you are my source of all things. I love you with all my heart, soul, mind and strength, and I will praise you forever.

Lord, you are gracious, merciful and full of compassion. You are Emmanuel, God with us, and you keep me and preserve me in all of my ways. You are the same yesterday, today and forever. Your goodness and mercy endures forever.

You are the Lord of Hosts. You are the King of glory. You are strong and mighty in battle. You are I AM that I AM. The only wise God. The true and living God. My Redeemer, my Healer, my Provider, my peace, my joy and I give you my all. Bless your holy name!

TESTIMONIES

Hi Minister Tiffany! I know that last week my cousin Malissa shared with you that I had gotten my dream job after years of being unemployed. I misunderstood at the time that it was just an invitation to the position. I had the phone interview last Wednesday, and she told me that she would get back to me in a few days. But I can say on today...I am the Assistant Office Manager at Fig Catering! They called me an hour ago and offered me the position. Monday through Friday 8-4! I start Thursday!

Nicole A.

Thanking and praising God for restoration, acceleration and elevation. God has taken my prayer life and blessed

me to understand more on how to pray and what to pray by the leading of the Holy Spirit.
Patricia S.

I believe it was on the pop-up scope done last week, where Minister Tiffany stated that hidden things would be revealed to us. The same day, the Lord revealed something to me regarding a family member and the next morning He gave me the opportunity to speak with them and fully address the demonic spirit in operation. What had been hidden was exposed, cast out and now teaching is going forth to help the individual renew their mind in this area.
Nicole M.

During my fast I got a better security paying job. THANK YOU LORD!
Diana D.

Allergies gone by day two of the twenty-one day fast.
Vicki E.

After being reinforced by Minister Tiffany that we are to command our blessings and that God is waiting on us to tell Him what we want, I received the following:

- Promotion on my job with substantial financial increase. Enough said!
- Moving into a new residence. God's timing is just perfect.
- Licensing with LWCC. (Not bragging, just my time, my turn). I was licensed with Monument Of Faith, and the devil tried to stop me. That alone makes this licensing so significant and beneficial to me. God is amazing!

I'm still waiting on the manifestation of one more miracle! It shall be done, in Jesus Name!

Sandy B.

In 2014, the school I worked for as a kindergarten teacher for five years closed. Due to having no success in finding another assignment here in Chicago, I decided to move to Kentucky in February 2015 to support my daughter and her family during her third pregnancy. During my stay, God spoke to me about an assignment/vision to pursue as well as He gave me the name of the assignment/vision. This assignment/vision also lead me to return to Chicago in February 2016.

Once I returned to Chicago, I immediately started looking for work. I started as an Uber and Lyft driver but in just a couple of weeks, I was hired as a daycare teacher assistant. The daycare assistant position assignment ended once school let out for the summer.

I decided to join the twenty-one day fast and prayer time with Minister Tiffany Jordan to seek God concerning a job, the vision, and other things I needed to hear from Him. In July I submitted my resume for a lead teacher position but wasn't called back.

A few days after starting the fast, that same company called me for the lead teaching position, and I was hired immediately without an interview! Praise God!
Joyce P.

My testimony is simply: I was in a cave. I CAME OUT!
Crystal M.

During the twenty-one day fast, I was believing for funds to attend the International Faith Conference at Living Word Christian Center (my first time attending this conference). God provided the money for travel, accommodations, cab fare, and then some. I even received some things for free. This was huge for me because I was experiencing somewhat of a drought in my finances. I am a tither. I was sowing. God always supplied my needs, but for some reason, I never had much extra left for anything beyond the basics and definitely not for travel (I'm from NC). I believe that participating in this fast and the daily prayers helped to fortify my faith. I have been experiencing increase ever since! To God be the glory. Special thanks to Minister Tiffany Jordan!

Vicki E.

During the fast, we received money that was due to us that had been held up. Also bills were decreased. We received a contract for a business endeavor in real estate. Our marriage is going really well. We are walking in agreement like never before. Our broken friendships have been restored. We are praying for favor in buying a house, vehicles, and to be blessed with children. This has been an awesome fast and time of prayer.

Alicia M.

I participated in the twenty-one day fast, sowed my seed in the ground according to the Word God gave you (Minister Tiffany), and I have been consistently watering my seed with the Word focusing on my finances. My daughter will be 21 on October 8th, and we planned a mini getaway to celebrate. I decided to use my faith for provision for the expenses, and God opened two doors of monetary blessings to finance the trip! It didn't come from my paycheck or checking account! The second praise report is that I just received an unexpected check in the mail from my pharmacy company showing I overpaid my co-pays in 2012! Praise God! God is faithful! One thing I did take note of is while I was in faith for provision, I was at peace and rest. I was not worrying or trying to make something happen for myself. I just continued to put God in remembrance of His Word. I thank you for your obedience to what God is calling you to do. Continued abundant blessings to you!

Monique H.

Easier flow while praying. Praying with confidence and strength.

Melvin J.

During this twenty-one day fast, I have rearranged my schedule to focus more of my time and attention to praying, meditating the Word of God and focusing more on my God assignment. I had been taking water pills to control blood pressure. On September 21st, the last day of the fast, I had a regularly scheduled doctor's appointment. My blood pressure was within normal levels. I had stopped taking the water pills on the first day of the fast.

Ruby E.

My husband and I have always filed our taxes every year like normal and on time. However, I recently received a letter in the mail from the IRS regarding our 2013 taxes and it stated that we owe $294.00 including late fees and penalties. Now we were not aware of any of this until the letter came in the mail. I talked to my brother-in-law about it who does our taxes, and I told him that we shouldn't have to pay anything and that the amount should be $0. So he glanced at our records and took it back to his office to further check into it. He thought maybe he had made an error.

I received a call from him telling me that we do not and I repeat we do not owe them anything because they owe us $56.00. I faxed all of the information along with the letter to them and, praise God, we're now waiting on a letter back from them along with my check. Thank you, Minister Tiffany, for your commitment and love for the Kingdom! Love you much. We are blessed!

Kenya W.

This twenty-one day fast rained on dry ground (me). I had been disconnected and oppressed by the enemy of my soul. This fast has strengthened me and caused me to use my praise and worship to reconnect to the Vine. My heart is full and my faith has been restored. I will continue to push and seek! I got my seek back. Talk about a blessing!

My little brother contacted me and shared with me his disconnection from family. He shared deep feelings of depression that 40-year-old black men have difficulty admitting to due to the stigma attached. We are now talking and planning to be more involved in each other's lives. Restoration, acceleration, and elevation are what God spoke during this fast. I believe this is just the beginning! Thank you again for your obedience! Pray for me as I pray for you! Grateful.

Francina S.

PRAYER OF SALVATION

God loves you just the way you are. He sent His only begotten Son Jesus to die for you and I. Say the prayer below and accept Him into your heart so that He can begin to lead you into the destiny that He has waiting for you.

Please pray this prayer:

Father God, I come to you now, just as I am. You know my life; and everything about me. Forgive me, Lord; I repent of my sins. I believe that Jesus Christ is the Son of God and that He died for my sins. I believe that on the third day He was raised from the dead. Lord, Jesus, I ask you now, to come inside of my heart, live in me and through me. From this day forth, I belong to you. Jesus, be Lord over my life. I believe and receive you right now, in Jesus' name, amen.

Scripture Reference:
Romans 10:9-10

BAPTISM OF THE HOLY SPIRIT

The baptism of the Holy Spirit is a gift from God. It is vital to the life of a believer in that the Holy Spirit comes upon you and endows you with power. The evidence of this infilling that is available to every believer is the manifestation of speaking in tongues.

Please pray this prayer:

Father, I ask you in the name of Jesus to fill me with the Holy Spirit. I step into the fullness of power that I desire, and that is my inheritance, in Jesus' name. I confess that I am a spirit-filled Christian and as I yield my vocal organs, I expect to speak in tongues, for the Spirit gives me utterance in the name of Jesus.

Scripture Reference:

Acts 1:8	Luke 11:13	John 14:14-16
Acts 2:4	1 Corinthians 14:2-15	
Acts 10:44-46	Jude 1:2	

ABOUT THE AUTHOR

Tiffany K. Jordan is an apostolic visionary leader. She is known as an intercessor, life and business coach, advisor and entrepreneur. Through prophetic insight and the anointing of God that is upon her life, she divinely positions people into their God-given assignments to maximize potential and dominate in their sphere of influence.

Tiffany is the Prayer Network Manager of The Joseph Center® and currently serves as a faculty member of the Joseph Business School. Tiffany has advised and provided prayer training, spiritual consultation, strategic planning and leadership development to ministries, business leaders and organizations worldwide.

Tiffany answered the call into ministry while working for a prestigious law firm in downtown Chicago. She started a Bible study during lunch hour, which led many to develop more intimate relationships with God. Signs, wonders and miracles followed the Word as she ministered during these meetings. The Lord led Tiffany to resign from her assignment at the law firm to prepare to serve full-time in ministry.

Tiffany graduated from Living Word School of Ministry and Missions and is a licensed minister. She is also a graduate of the Joseph Business School. Tiffany was formerly the Prayer Ministry Coordinator at Living Word Christian Center pastored by Dr. Bill Winston.

She has authored the book *Life Without Limits: 52 Biblical Principles to Reach Your Prophetic Destiny.* Through Tiffany's transformational leadership, teachings and prophetic counsel, many lives and organizations have been repositioned and catapulted into greater influence, productivity and profitability. Tiffany resides in the Chicagoland area and is the mother of two daughters.

Connect with Minister Tiffany K. Jordan on Social Media

/TiffanyKJordan

/Tiffany-K-Jordan

/TiffanyKJordan_

/TiffanyKJordan_

www.tiffanyjordan.co
www.tiffanyjordanministries.org

<u>Other Resources by Minister Tiffany</u>

Life Without Limits
52 Biblical Principles to Reach Your Prophetic Destiny

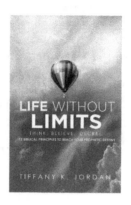

Thanks for reading! Please add a short review on Amazon and let me know your thoughts!

If this book was a blessing to you, please recommend it to or share it with a friend.